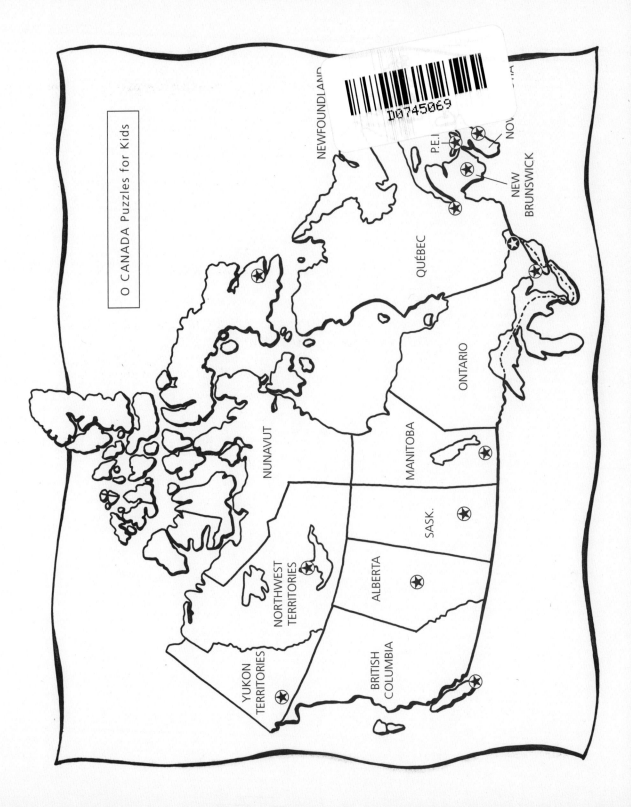

O CANADA Puzzles for Kids

For our favourite puzzle fan
Audrey Porter

O CANADA

PUZZLES

for KIDS

Jesse **Ross** &
Ruth **Porter**

Illustrated by Anne **DeGrace**

BLUEFIELD BOOKS

O Canada Puzzles for Kids
Copyright © 2001 by Jesse Ross and Ruth Porter. All rights reserved.

Published by
Bluefield Books
Gr. 12, C. 9, RR 1, Winlaw, B.C.   V0G 2J0   1-800-296-6955

Distributed by
Raincoast Books
9050 Shaughnessy Street, Vancouver, B.C.   V6P 6E5   604-323-7100

NATIONAL LIBRARY OF CANADA CATALOGUING IN PUBLICATION DATA
Ross, Jesse, 1986-
    O Canada puzzles for kids

  ISBN 1-894404-06-8

  1. Canada—Miscellanea—Juvenile literature. 2. Puzzles—Juvenile literature. I. Porter, Ruth, 1957- II. Title.
FC58.R67 2001   j971   C2001-910703-X
F1008.2.R67 2001

Interior illustrations by Anne DeGrace
Cover and interior design by Jim Brennan

For more information on the Nova Scotian folk art portrayed on the cover, please visit the Black Sheep Gallery website at www.blacksheepart.com

Printed in Canada

5 4 3 2

Contents

Contents (continued)

Puzzles

Home Plates

The goal here is to match the province or territory with their license plate slogan. But it's not as easy as it sounds — two share the same slogan, one province has two, while another has no text but features the drawing of a ship.

Alberta	Friendly
British Columbia	A World of Difference
Manitoba	The Klondike
New Brunswick	Explore Canada's Arctic
Newfoundland and Labrador	Beautiful
Northwest Territories	Land of Living Skies
Nova Scotia	Canada's Ocean Playground
Nunavut	Confederation Bridge
Ontario	Wild Rose Country
Prince Edward Island	Explore Canada's Arctic
Quebec	Birthplace of Confederation
Saskatchewan	Yours to Discover
Yukon Territory	Je me souviens

Dream Teams

We've mixed a couple of phony names into the following list of professional sports teams — can you guess which two they are?

Toronto Lynx
Ottawa Rebel
Edmonton Trappers
Montreal Alouettes

Saint John Flames
Regina Redcaps
Vancouver Breakers
Brandon Hurricanes

Multiple Mounties

Two of our Mounties are identical, while the remaining ones are all a bit different. Which two are the same?

1   2   3   4   5   6

Common Ground

What do the following people, places or things have in common?

1. Toothpaste, ice cream, and cough syrup?
    a) they are the top three selling grocery items in Canada;
    b) they all contain Irish moss, a seaweed found on P.E.I. beaches;
    c) they're the titles of Bryan Adams' last three albums.

2. Marc Garneau, Julie Payette, and Chris Hadfield?
    a) they are all members of the comedy troupe "Air Farce";
    b) they are all Canadians astronauts;
    c) they are all Canadian peace-keepers.

3. Basketball, snowmobiles, and zippers?
    a) they were all invented by Canadians;
    b) they have all been briefly banned in
       Nova Scotia;
    c) the game of Snow-Basketball played
       while driving snowmobiles is sponsored
       by the Canadian Zipper Company.

4. Larry Walker, Ryan Dempster, and Matt Stairs?
    a) these three Ontario friends invented the game Trivial Pursuit;
    b) they are all former premiers of Alberta;
    c) they're all Canadians playing Major League Baseball.

5. Angela Cutrone, Mark McKoy, and Larry Cain?
    a) they've all won Olympic gold medals for Canada;
    b) they're all Canadian children's authors;
    c) all of them are multi-millionaires living in Canada.

6. The Canadian quarter, dime, and fifty-cent piece?
   a) they are made of 100% nickel;
   b) they were coins introduced into Canada by Irish immigrants in 1856;
   c) they are due to be phased out of circulation in 2010.

7. The video games NBA Street, SSX Tricky, and NHL 2002?
   a) they were all developed by EA (Electronic Arts) Canada;
   b) they were Canada's top-selling video games in 2001;
   c) Wayne Gretzky is a secret character in all of the games.

8. Lake Manitoba, Okanagan Lake, and Lake Winnipegosis?
   a) they are all located in Manitoba;
   b) powerboats aren't allowed, only canoes and sailboats;
   c) they all claim to be home to sea monsters.

9. The Trans-Canada Highway, Confederation Bridge, and the Rideau Canal?
   a) they all hold world records;
   b) they were all completed in 1978;
   c) they have all been named World Heritage Sites.

Record-Makers

Can you match these world-famous Canadian athletes with their accomplishments?

Elvis Stojko _____   Simon Whitfield _____

Sandra Schmirler _____   Bruny Surin _____

Catriona Le May Doan _____ Donovan Bailey _____

1. This sprinter made it to the finals of the 100 Metres of the World Track and Field Championships five times in a row, winning two silver medals.

2. After winning the gold in triathlon at the 2000 Olympic Games, this B.C.-based athlete went on to carry the Canadian flag during the closing ceremonies.

3. This speed skater has been on the Canadian National Team since 1988 and currently holds the world record for 500 metres. This Saskatoon-born athlete won a gold and a bronze in speed skating at the 1998 Olympics.

4. Before sadly passing away in March 2000, this curling skip won a gold at the 1998 Olympic Games, and also won three World Championships.

5. This world-famous figure skater won two silver medals at the Olympics, and was the first to complete a quad jump in competition.

6. Former world record holder in the 100 metres sprint, this gold-medal winning Olympian retired after the 2001 World Championships in Edmonton.

You Live Where?

We've hidden 18 unusual place names in this word search; they're written either forwards or backwards, and placed horizontally, vertically or diagonally. When you've finished, 24 letters will be left over that spell out the names of two Canadian communities — when combined with the leftover letters on page 13, they make a seasonal set.

```
M  S  H  S  I  N  A  P  S  H
P  A  Y  L  E  K  I  L  R  E
I  N  G  N  I  D  A  E  R  A
G  S  U  N  D  O  W  N  O  D
V  C  I  N  E  M  A  V  R  Q
A  U  L  L  E  T  B  S  R  U
Y  A  L  U  N  T  A  S  I  A
U  M  N  C  W  I  T  I  M  R
P  U  G  W  A  S  H  L  S  T
F  O  G  O  L  N  O  B  L  E
K  C  I  U  Q  V  A  N  D  R
D  A  N  C  E  Y  L  L  I  S
```

BATH (NB)	LAWN (NF)	QUICK (BC)
BLISS (ON)	LIKELY (BC)	READING (ON)
CINEMA (BC)	LOVE (QC)	SILLY (QC)
DANCE (ON)	MAGNET (MB)	SPANISH (ON)
FOGO (NF)	MIRROR (AB)	SUNDOWN (MB)
HEADQUARTERS (BC)	PUGWASH (NS)	VULCAN (AB)

_ _ _ _ _ _ _   _ _ _ _ _ _ _ (PEI)   _ _ _ _ _ _ _   _ _ _ _ _ _ _ (NF)

Note: the provincial abbreviations are listed for your information only — they're not part of the puzzle.

O Hungry? O Canada!

Twenty of Canada's tastiest place names are hidden in this puzzle; they're written either forwards or backwards, and placed horizontally, vertically or diagonally. At the bottom of the page, fill in the remaining 20 letters in order, to complete the set.

```
W  I  H  C  I  W  D  N  A  S
Y  N  S  T  C  O  N  I  O  N
L  R  K  E  R  R  T  U  N  C
L  C  R  L  A  E  R  E  C  K
E  A  O  E  N  S  K  O  O  C
B  R  F  H  B  O  A  V  E  U
S  R  D  S  E  W  U  L  M  B
Y  O  N  I  R  C  A  E  T  R
P  T  A  N  R  M  I  R  E  A
I  E  R  R  Y  P  R  R  T  T
H  L  G  A  A  R  A  G  U  S
C  N  D  G  N  I  K  O  O  C
```

BELLY River (AB)	EGG Lake (SK)	RICE Lake (ON)
CARROT River (SK)	FRY Lake (ON)	SALT River (AB)
CEREAL (AB)	GARNISH (NF)	SANDWICH Bay (NF)
CHIP Lake (AB)	GRAND FORKS (BC)	STARBUCK (MB)
COOK'S Harbour (NF)	NUT Lake (SK)	STRAWBERRY Hill (BC)
COOKING Lake (AB)	ONION Lake (SK)	SUGAR Lake (BC)
CRANBERRY Portage (MB)	PIE Island (ON)	

_ _ _ _ _ _ _   _ _ _ _ _ (NT)   _ _ _ _ _ _ _ _ _ _ _ _ (BC)

Note: For this puzzle, only the words in capitals are included, i.e. for STRAWBERRY Hill (BC), only STRAWBERRY is hidden. Once again, provincial abbreviations are included here for information only.

On Land and Sea

ACROSS

1 The sound that owls make
3 Large mammal, often mistaken for an elk
7 Spartan, Delicious and MacIntosh are all types of _____
8 The main form of long-distance transportation in northern Canada
9 Popular Canadian children's nature magazine
10 You might see one of these on a hot summer's day in Canada's only desert near Osoyoos, B.C.
11 This popular game is often used to raise money for charity
13 These wild herbivores are sometimes kept as pets; they love garden greens
15 Polar and Kermode
16 O Canada is our national _____
19 Bannock, Whole Wheat and French are types of _____
20 If it's 1:30 p.m. in Newfoundland, what time is it in Toronto?
21 These small but powerful boats move large freighters through the St. Lawrence Seaway

DOWN

2 Kenneth _____, children's author, whose books include a popular fiction series featuring bats
4 This kind of stone is often used by the Inuit for carving
5 The NHL team based in Ottawa
6 These whales can be found year-round in the St. Lawrence River
8 Alligator Pie, by Dennis Lee, is a _____ as well as the title of a book
12 The Titanic hit one of these and sunk
14 What you need to solve this puzzle
17 Deux, in English
18 What sled dog drivers sometimes shout at their dogs
19 You might find this night-flyer in a cave

On Land and Sea

What Am I?

Can you figure out what these clues point to? Try to get the answer in as few clues as possible.

#1 _____

a) I used to be home to a military post, but now I'm a world famous vacation spot.

b) I'm known as the Honeymoon Capital of the World.

c) For over a century, people have been going over me in barrels, large rubber balls, and other contraptions.

d) After seeing me, author Mark Twain said, "Although it was wonderful to see all that water tumbling down, it would be even more wonderful to see all that water tumbling up."

#2

a) I've been called one of the world's greatest mysteries.

b) For over 200 years people have searched below me. So far, they've found such things as metal, cement, scissors, leather shoes, a human hand, and a rock inscribed with mysterious symbols.

c) I'm a very small island off the coast of Nova Scotia.

d) It is believed that pirate's treasure has been buried beneath me, but even though millions of dollars has been spent trying to find it, to this day no one has.

#3 _____

a) I was bought for $50 in 1892, but now I'm worth millions.

b) I have been lost, stolen, used as a potty and featured in television ads.

c) I'm the oldest trophy in North American professional sports.

d) Millions of people have dreamt of holding me, but only one team per year has this honour.

Spot the Difference: Camping

There are at least 20 differences between these two pages; how many can you spot?

It's a Numbers Game

Match the statements on the left, with the numbers on the right.

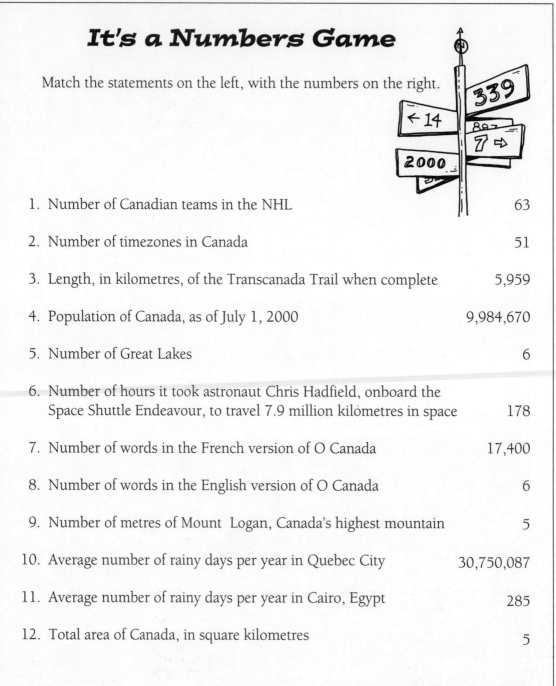

1. Number of Canadian teams in the NHL 63

2. Number of timezones in Canada 51

3. Length, in kilometres, of the Transcanada Trail when complete 5,959

4. Population of Canada, as of July 1, 2000 9,984,670

5. Number of Great Lakes 6

6. Number of hours it took astronaut Chris Hadfield, onboard the Space Shuttle Endeavour, to travel 7.9 million kilometres in space 178

7. Number of words in the French version of O Canada 17,400

8. Number of words in the English version of O Canada 6

9. Number of metres of Mount Logan, Canada's highest mountain 5

10. Average number of rainy days per year in Quebec City 30,750,087

11. Average number of rainy days per year in Cairo, Egypt 285

12. Total area of Canada, in square kilometres 5

Lost Letters

Add one letter to each line which will end the left word and start the right word, changing both into Canadian cities or towns. The missing letters, when read from top to bottom, spell the name of one of our largest mammals.

CHETICAM ____ ERTH

TRUR ____ SHAWA

LAVA ____ ONDON

KENOR ____ BBOTSFORD

BIGGA ____ ICHMOND

WEB ____ ADDECK

LACHIN ____ DMONTON

SARNI ____ JAX

GANDE ____ EGINA

Lights... Camera... Action!

Match the Canadian actor on the left with the movie they were in on the right.

Keanu Reeves	Mr. Magoo
Jim Carrey	The Mummy
Mike Myers	Superman
Neve Campbell	Speed
William Shatner	Red Planet
Brendan Fraser	Freddy Got Fingered
Carrie-Anne Moss	How the Grinch Stole Christmas
Dan Aykroyd	Scream 2
Leslie Nielsen	Austin Powers
Margot Kidder	Blues Brothers 2000
Rick Moranis	Star Trek: The Final Frontier
Tom Green	The Skulls
Joshua Jackson	Honey I Shrunk the Kids

Odd One Out

Each group of words listed below has an error. Find the one word you think doesn't belong with the others.

ISLANDS
P.E.I.,   Baffin,   Centre,   Red Deer

LAKES
Biche,   Great Bear,   Lacrosse,   Meech

RIVERS
Pippen,   Skeena,   Saskatchewan,   Mann

MOUNTAINS
Logan,   Leisure,   St. John's,   Selkirk

PARKS
Fathom Five,   Point Pelee,   Sirmilik,   Chitimani

PRIME MINISTERS
Preston Manning,   Joe Clark,   Kim Campbell,   Louis St. Laurent

NATIVE GROUPS
Wakashan,   Haida,   Mic Mac,   Inukstituk

BIRDS
Chickaree,   Gyrfalcon,   Calliope,   Phoebe

DEER
Mule,   Antler,   Whitetail,   Red

Olympic Games

1. The 1976 Montreal Summer Olympic Games were plagued by problems. Which of the following things did *not* happen?

   a) 24 out of 116 nations boycotted the Games, for various reasons;

   b) the Games cost Montreal over one billion dollars more than they had expected;

   c) the volleyball arena wasn't completed in time, so the men's and women's volleyball events had to be cancelled.

2. The star of the 1976 Summer Games in Montreal was 14-year-old Romanian gymnast Nadia Comaneci. Why?

   a) she scored seven perfect 10's in gymnastics;

   b) she was the first female to compete in the pommel horse event;

   c) after suffering a terrible tumble off the pommel horse, she went on to win gold in rhythmic gymnastics while wearing a full-leg cast.

3. At the 1988 Calgary Winter Games, Britain's Eddie "The Eagle" Edwards became an over-night celebrity (mainly because he was so bad), and captured the hearts of people around the world. What event was he competing in?

   a) luge;

   b) figure skating;

   c) ski jumping.

4. Robert Esmie, a member of Canada's 4 x 100 metre relay team that won gold at the Atlanta Summer Games in 1996, shaved what words into his hair before the race?

     a) Blast Off;

     b) Eat my Dust;

     c) We're #1.

5. Glenroy Gilbert, another member of the 1996 men's gold-medal relay team, has competed in three Summer Olympics plus one Winter Games in Lillehammer, Norway. What was his winter sport?

     a) basketball;

     b) 4-man bobsled;

     c) speed skating.

6. Canada is bidding to host the 2010 Winter Olympics. If the International Olympic Committee awards the Games to Canada, in which city would they be held?

     a) Quebec City;

     b) Vancouver/Whister;

     c) Toronto.

Wild Canada

Here you'll find the names of six animals or birds which all start from the middle C. The names are found in any direction, and rarely in a straight line.

B	I	M	T	E
O	K	R	O	Y
U	N	A	O	N
U	H	**C**	E	K
M	I	A	R	E
P	C	L	N	D
T	L	K	A	I

Dollars and Cents

Do you know what coins these illustrations are featured on? Write its name under the image.

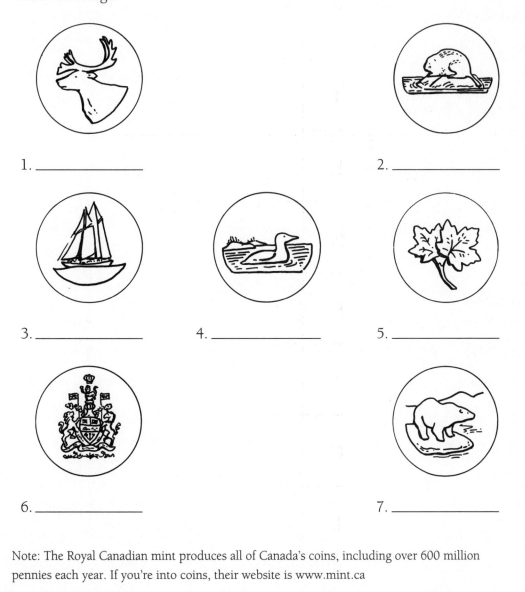

1. _____

2. _____

3. _____

4. _____

5. _____

6. _____

7. _____

Note: The Royal Canadian mint produces all of Canada's coins, including over 600 million pennies each year. If you're into coins, their website is www.mint.ca

What's My Sport?

What sport are these athletes best known for?

ACROSS

1 Steve Nash
4 Alison Sydor
6 Carolyn Brunet
7 Marnie McBean
8 Lorie Kane
10 Daniel Igali
13 Attila and Tamas Buday
14 Colleen Jones
15 Sebastien Lareau
16 Hayley Wickenheiser

DOWN

1 Mike Strange
2 Simon Whitfield
3 Colin Doyle
5 Melanie Turgeon
9 Lui Passaglia
11 Craig Forrest
12 Jonathan Powers

What's My Sport?

Prime Time

Many of the familiar faces you see on TV are Canadian. Fill in the blanks by choosing one of the clues at the bottom of page 30.

1. Caroline _____ plays the aunt of a witch on "_____ The Teenage Witch."

2. _____ B. Davis, the Cigarette-Smoking Man, is a villain on "The _____."

3. _____ Chalke co-stars in the new comedy "_____."

4. Matthew _____, plays Chandler on "_____."

5. _____ Jones, one of the two female co-hosts on the comedy news show "This _____ has 22 _____."

6. _____ Lindros, after retiring from the NHL, now hosts "Be A _____, The NHLPA Show."

7. William _____ played the original Captain on "_____ _____."

8. Jonathan _____ is the host of "_____", a show named after himself.

9. _____ Jackson co-stars in "_____ Creek", along with Michelle Williams, James Van der Beek and Kate Holmes.

10. Alex _____ is the game show host on "_____."

11. _____ Mochrie co-stars in the improv comedy show hosted by Drew Carey, "Whose _____ Is It Anyway?"

_____

Brett	Player
Cathy	Rhea
Colin	Sabrina
Dawson's	Sarah
Friends	Scrubs
Hour	Shatner
Jeopardy!	Star
Jonovision	Torrens
Joshua	Trebeck
Line	Trek
Minutes	William
Perry	X-Files

Confused Cities

The following sets of letters are mixed-up Canadian cities. See if you can unravel them — but beware, each has one extra letter.

1. C K T O R V I A I   _____

2. R O T S O T N O   _____

3. L A E R N A O M T   _____

4. G Y C A R L A O   _____

5. C N T M O N O N   _____

6. A F A H X I A L   _____

7. T H I W O S E R H E S _____

8. N A D O G R E   _____

9. P I N T G E N I W   _____

Unravel the nine extra letters to discover the name of both a great pie and a great city.

____ ____ ____ ____ ____ ____ ____ ____

Juggled Geography

We've mixed up the names of 16 islands, peaks, bays, rivers, etc.
Can you sort them out?

Okanagan Current
Digby Jaw
Thousand River
Bay of Louise
Mont Circle
Gros George
Point Bay
Georgian Mountain

Moose Morne
Peace Islands
Swift Valley
Riding Bay
Hudson Pelee
Prince Neck
Arctic Tremblant
Lake Fundy

_____

_____   _____

_____   _____

_____   _____

_____   _____

Across Canada

Fit the words below into their proper places in the puzzle squares. Each word is used only once. We've started you off by filling in RED.

3 letters

FUR

~~RED~~

YOU

4 letters

DEER

DRIP

FLAG

GOLD

KITE

PARK

SLED

SNOW

STAR

YAWN

YETI

5 letters

CROPS

FERRY

GROUP

METRE

POLAR

SIOUX

SKIER

TROUT

BIRTH

6 letters

ACORNS

GIGGLE

HOCKEY

HUBBLE

HUDSON

MUSEUM

RABBIT

7 letters

ALBERTA

MUSKRAT

NIAGARA

SPECIAL

8 letters

LABRADOR

MOUNTIES

PROVINCE

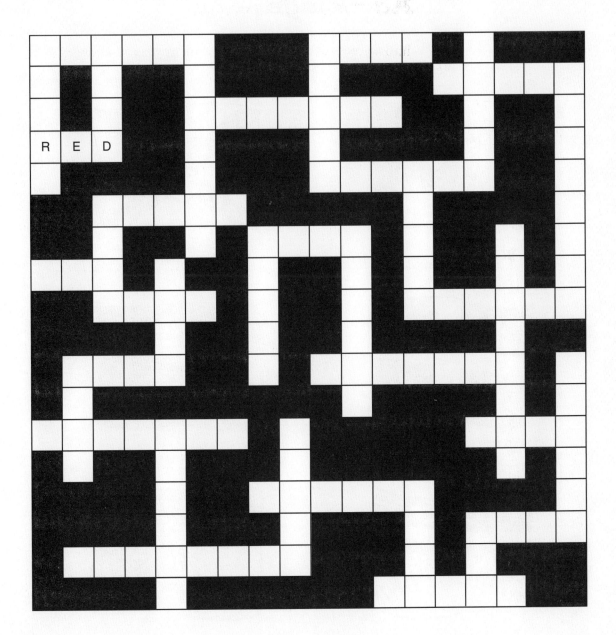

Flags

Here are 13 flags of the provinces and territories. How many do you know?

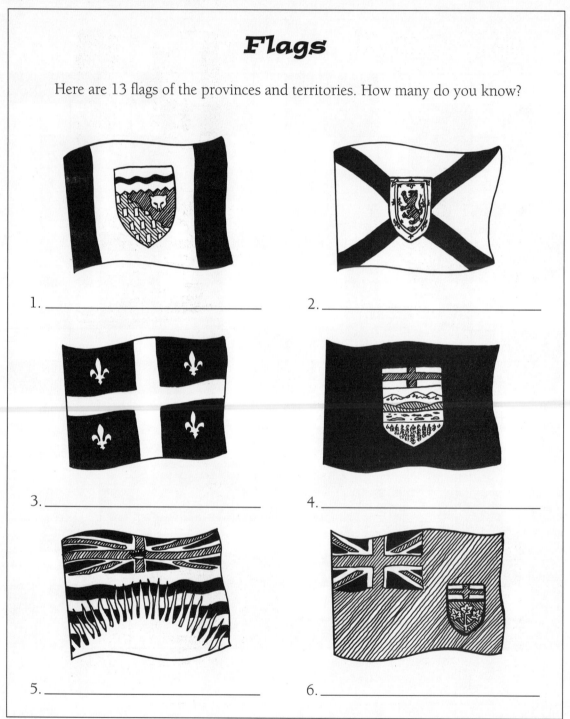

1. _____

2. _____

3. _____

4. _____

5. _____

6. _____

7. _____

8. _____

9. _____

10. _____

11. _____

12. _____

13. _____

Wild Canada #2

Here you'll find the names of six mammals which all start from the middle M. The names are found in any direction, and rarely in a straight line.

O	O	M	Y	B	E	T
S	E	K	R	M	R	O
P	O	S	U	A	M	K
U	L	O	**M**	O	T	S
S	K	E	I	A	U	T
S	T	M	O	N	U	S
R	I	N	K	T	K	E

Famous Canadians

Below are the names of 20 well-known Canadians. We've hidden 19 of them in this wordsearch; they're written forwards or backwards, and hidden horizontally, vertically or diagonally. Can you also find the one name that isn't in the puzzle?

H	K	E	P	N	J	E	R	H	C
Y	C	R	E	O	E	Y	C	R	A
A	O	O	L	W	U	L	A	O	S
N	S	S	L	A	H	N	L	G	S
K	E	N	E	L	L	Y	D	E	I
O	H	J	T	N	U	T	R	R	E
V	T	M	I	B	O	C	I	G	A
I	D	P	E	R	R	Y	C	C	S
C	E	S	R	F	O	J	K	A	E
A	P	E	L	L	G	S	I	M	M
G	N	A	T	A	O	B	S	M	A
S	A	L	E	M	J	K	E	O	J

Kwaku BOATANG, high jumper
JAMES Cameron, director
CASSIE Campbell, hockey player
JIM Carrey, actor
JEAN Chretien, politician
ED THE SOCK, MuchMusic puppet VJ
NELLY Furtado, singer/songwriter
Marie-Louise GAY, writer/illustrator
Todd MACCULLOCH, basketball player
Roy MACGREGOR, writer

RICK Mercer, comedian
David PELLETIER, figure skater
Matthew PERRY, actor
Dick POUND, Olympic director
Jesse ROSS, hero
JOE Sakic, hockey player
Jamie SALE, figure skater
ELLEN Schwartz, writer
Jonathan TORRENS, TV host
Weird-Al YANKOVIC, singer

Note: For this puzzle, only the names in capitals are included, i.e. for Kwaku BOATANG, only BOATANG is hidden.

Puzzling Pictures

These drawings represent the names of provinces, territories, cities and towns across Canada. Some of them are two words. Can you guess what they are?

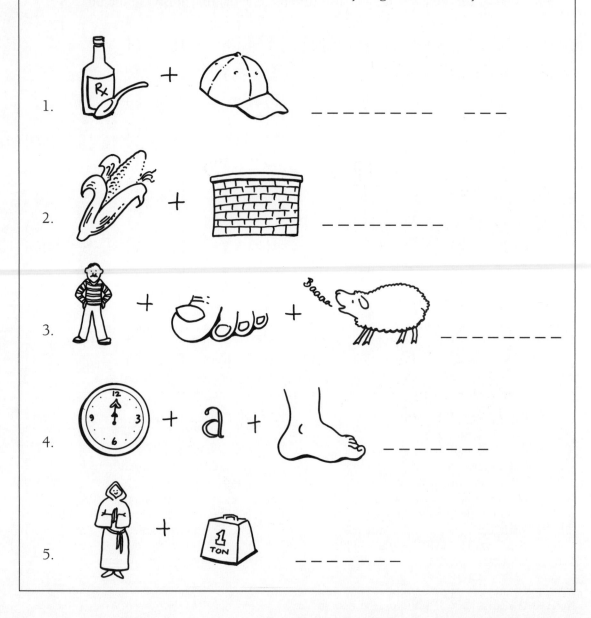

1. _ _ _ _ _ _ _ _   _ _ _

2. _ _ _ _ _ _ _ _

3. _ _ _ _ _ _ _ _ _

4. _ _ _ _ _ _ _

5. _ _ _ _ _ _ _

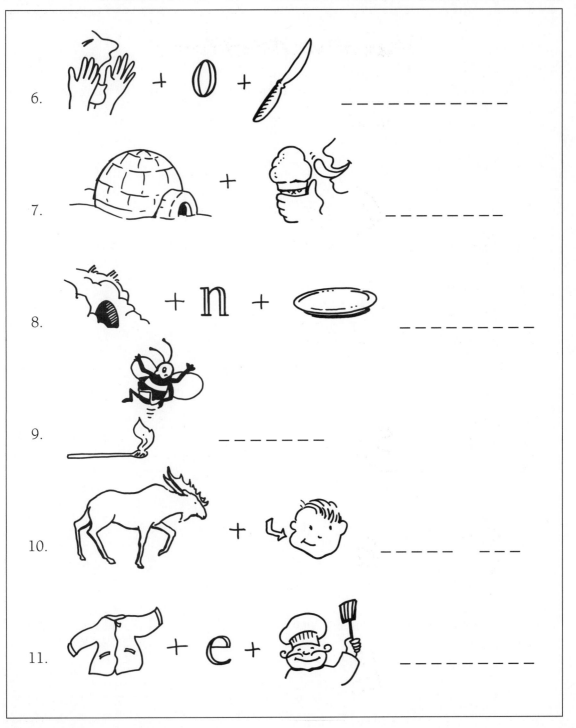

6. _ _ _ _ _ _ _ _ _ _ _ _

7. _ _ _ _ _ _ _ _

8. _ _ _ _ _ _ _ _ _

9. _ _ _ _ _ _ _

10. _ _ _ _ _ _ _ _

11. _ _ _ _ _ _ _ _ _

Who Am I?

Can you figure out who these clues point to? Try to get the answer in as few clues as possible.

#1 _____

a) If you had met me, you would have to be at least 125 years old.

b) But that doesn't mean you don't see my name everywhere.

c) I helped give "birth" to Canada.

d) You can find my face on the new ten dollar bill.

#2 _____

a) I grew up in Coquitlam, B.C.

b) I was an athlete in high school; basketball was one of my favourite sports.

c) In the spring and summer of 1980, I attracted huge crowds wherever I went, raising millions of dollars.

d) In my honour, each September Canadians run, bike and walk to raise money for cancer research.

#3 _____

a) I was born in Lac Beauport, Quebec in 1972.

b) I've won two world championship gold medals for Canada.

c) I was the first woman to sign a professional contract with a National Hockey League team.

d) In 1992, I played goal for one period in an NHL exhibition game with the Tampa Bay Lightning, stopping 7 of 9 shots.

Double Dribble

Two of these soccer players are identical, while the remaining ones are all a bit different. Which two are the same?

1   2   3   4   5   6

_____   _____

Puzzling Letters

The object of this puzzle is to figure out the three words listed at the bottom — something you'll find on a map of Canada. We've given you four clues. Fill in as many as you can, then transfer the letters from the clues to the numbers at the bottom. For example, if you think the first letter in the first clue is an A, then you'd fill in A where you see 6 in the mystery phrase.

Clues

a) __ __ __ __ __ __   What happens when you don't eat
    6   5   12   2   9   14

b) __ __ __ __ __   Not small
    7   4   2   1   10

c) __ __ __   We travel in herds across the west
    3   11   13

d) __ __ __ __   A story or fable
    5   8   7   14

___ ___ ___ ___ ___   ___ ___ ___ ___ ___   ___ ___ ___ ___
 1   2   3   4   5   6   7   8   9   10   11   12   13   14

Lost Letters #2

Add one letter to each line which will end the left word and start the right word, changing both into Canadian cities or towns. The missing letters when read from top to bottom, name a tasty favourite.

CHATA ____ INTO

WABAN ____ MHURST

CAR ____ OWELL RIVER

HUL ____ ETHBRIDGE

CAPE WOLF ____ STEVAN

AMO ____ UDBURY

GRIMSB ____ AHK

KALADA ____ ED DEER

BAIE-COMEA ____ NITY

NAKUS ____ ORTAGE LA PRAIRIE

Your Choice

1. Joe Louis cakes are yummy cream-filled cakes. The first ones were made by the Vachon bakery of St. Marie, Quebec and named after:

    a) then prime minister Louis St. Laurent and Quebec premier Joseph Sauve;

    b) Joe Louis the champion heavyweight boxer;

    c) the baker's sons Joseph and Louis.

2. The world's largest concentration of pingos, about 1450, occurs in the Mackenzie Delta area of the Northwest Territories. What are pingos?

    a) a type of shore bird;

    b) a cone-shaped hill;

    c) the only Arctic-dwelling species of penguin.

3. Over one million people witness Caribana each year. What is it?

    a) the yearly migration of caribou from Nunavut into northern Manitoba;

    b) a Caribbean/Canadian carnival held each summer in Toronto;

    c) an ice climbing competition held each January at Montmorency Falls in Quebec.

4. On September 7, 1991, the city of Calgary suffered extensive damage. The cost of repairs totalled more than $400 million and damaged 65, 000 automobiles. What was the cause?

    a) a wildfire;

    b) a tornado;

    c) a hailstorm.

5. Who were the Group of Seven?

   a) the original seven NHL teams;

   b) early 20th century painters;

   c) the seven official languages of Canada.

6. Etienne Desmarteau won Canada's first gold medal in 1904. What sport did he win it in? (There used to be some crazy sports in the early days of the Olympics!)

   a) hammer throw;

   b) long-distance spitting;

   c) live pig chasing.

7. If you're standing with your toes in the Gulf of St. Lawrence in Tadoussac, Quebec, then hop in a plane and head west for 3000 kms, you'll end up in:

   a) Maple Creek, Saskatchewan;

   b) Banff National Park;

   c) the middle of Lake Winnipeg.

8. Canada has the longest coastline in the world. If it was stretched out in a straight line it would:

   a) stretch from the North Pole to the South Pole;

   b) circle the earth three times;

   c) reach two-thirds of the way to the moon.

Spot the Difference: Hockey

There are at least 20 differences between these two pages; how many can you spot?

Across Canada #2

Fit the words below into their proper places in the puzzle squares. Each word is used only once. We've started you off by filling in COLONIST.

4 letters
FISH
FLAG
FORT
GOLD
HERD
LAND
MAPS
UNIT

5 letters
ATLAS
BLOOD
HAIDA
HURON
INUIT
L'ANSE
MEECH
NORTH

6 letters
ABSORB
BATTLE
BERING
CHURCH
EQUALS
FRANCE
MICMAC
OUTLAW
SALMON
TREATY

7 letters
CITADEL
NEUTRAL
OJIBWAY
OUTPOST
PASSAGE
VOYAGES

8 letters
~~COLONIST~~
IROQUOIS
SETTLERS

C O L O N I S T

Boggling Letters

The letters below spell out Vancouver. How many words of four letters or more can you make using these nine letters?

VAN
COU
VER

If you enjoyed this puzzle, try SASKATCHEWAN; we found over 100 words of four or more letters!

Puzzling Letters #2

The object of this puzzle is to figure out the three words listed at the bottom — something to listen to. We've given you four clues. Fill in as many as you can, then transfer the letters from the clues to the numbers at the bottom.

a) ___ ___ ___ ___
   10   2   5   9

The 7th word in "O Canada."

b) ___ ___ ___ ___ ___
   15 7 13 8 3

Melanie Turgeon or Nicolas Fontaine

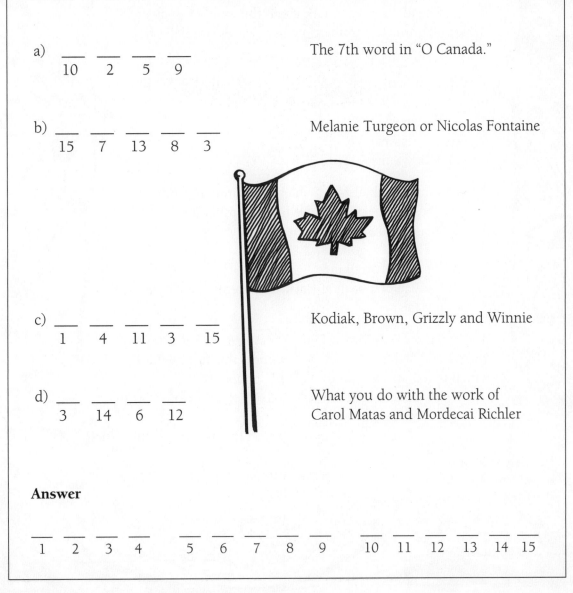

c) ___ ___ ___ ___ ___
   1   4 11 3 15

Kodiak, Brown, Grizzly and Winnie

d) ___ ___ ___ ___
   3 14 6 12

What you do with the work of
Carol Matas and Mordecai Richler

Answer

___ ___ ___ ___   ___ ___ ___ ___ ___   ___ ___ ___ ___ ___ ___
 1   2   3   4   5   6   7   8   9   10 11 12 13 14 15

Weather Wonders

Canadians love to talk about the weather — from winter blizzards to summertime heat waves, we definitely have lots to talk about.

1. Which was the only Canadian city to make the list of the top 10 coldest places in the world?
    a) Churchill, MB;
    b) Whitehorse, YK;
    c) Yellowknife, NT.

2. In a July 1996 hailstorm which hit Winnipeg and Calgary the damages were close to $300 million. Approximately how big were the hailstones?
    a) the size of a golf ball;
    b) the size of an orange;
    c) the size of a peanut, but with exceptionally dense ice crystals.

3. On the night of March 29th, 1848 Niagara Falls stopped. Over 5,000 sightseers arrived to witness this rare event which lasted for two full days. What happened?
    a) ice jams in Lake Erie blocked off the flow of water to the Niagara River;
    b) an intense cold snap resulted in the freezing of the falls;
    c) a U.S. plan to divert water to increase the flow to the American Falls backfired.

4. The 1998 ice storm that hit central and eastern Canada brought down enough power and telephone wires to:
   a) wrap around the world three times;
   b) power all the cities in the United States;
   c) stretch from the North Pole to the South Pole.

5. Which event did Canadians vote as the top weather story of the 20th century?
   a) The dustbowl of the 1930s;
   b) the 1997 flooding of Manitoba's Red River;
   c) the 1998 ice storm.

6. Canada's snowiest city gets an average of 415 cm of snow each year. (If this snow fell all at once it would be the same height as Vince Carter standing on top of Antonio Davis. What city is it?
   a) Jasper, AB;
   b) Sept-Iles, QC;
   c) Norman Wells, NT.

7. Cake, grease, glass, slush, pancake, shuga and frazil are all terms for snow.
   True   or   False

8. Chinook is a native word meaning *snow eater.*
   True   or   False

The Doors

You are taking your first piano lesson with Miss Violet Plant. You've followed the directions to her street but can't remember her exact house number. Follow the clues listed below to help you decide which of these six doors she lives at.

a) she is, true to her name, a lover of flowers;

b) she doesn't live in the Maritimes — in fact she doesn't even like to be near the ocean;

c) the number of her house cannot be evenly divided by seven;

d) she isn't fond of visitors;

e) but she loves her cats.

Violet Plant's house number is _____

Inter—National?

When is Denmark not in Europe? When it is in Nova Scotia — along with Borneo, Tangier and Damascus! And did you know that you can find Togo, Madrid and Stonehenge in southern Saskatchewan? Or how about Finland, Siberia and Zurich in Ontario? And, to top it off, we found the British Empire on the northwestern tip of Ellesmere Island in Nunavut.

More Choices

1. Why does the Confederation Bridge (which connects PEI to New Brunswick) have a curve in it?
>   a) so drivers won't fall asleep crossing this 12.9 km-long bridge;
>   b) when the bridge was being constructed, as an April Fools prank, the nightcrew added a curve;
>   c) each August the bridge is the site of the Maritime Nascar Race, and the race organizers required a curve in the track.

2. In the spring of 2001, the show Popstars created an all-girl Canadian pop band. What was the band called?
>   a) Girl Street;
>   b) Sugar Jones;
>   c) Cream 'n Sugar.

3. Each year gardeners flock to Desmond, Ontario to take part in:
>   a) Canada's largest flower festival;
>   b) the gardeners' annual Hall-of-Fame banquet;
>   c) a manure festival.

4. St. Paul, AB is home to the world's:
>   a) tallest cow statue;
>   b) only flying saucer launch pad;
>   c) largest hockey stick.

5. Many Canadian place names come from Native words; for instance, Gaspé comes from *gaspeg* meaning:
>   a) tongue sticking out;
>   b) where the world ends;
>   c) home of big fish.

6. Bernard Landry, now premier of Quebec, once proposed an increase of $11 million to remedy what provincial shortage?
   a) nursing staff;
   b) highway snow-removal equipment;
   c) clowns.

7. Outhouse is the most common type of _____ on Long Island, NS?
   a) bathroom facility;
   b) building;
   c) surname or last name.

8. Pile o' Bones was the name first given to which Canadian city?
   a) Regina, SK;
   b) Brandon, MB;
   c) Drumheller, AB.

9. Each May, Ottawa hosts the Tulip Festival. Every year, the Netherlands send 10,000 tulips bulbs to the festival. Why?
   a) one tulip for every Dutch immigrant living in Canada;
   b) the Netherlands is a small country, and they don't have room for all their bulbs;
   c) during WWII, Canada provided a safe haven for the Queen of the Netherlands.

Canadiana

ACROSS

1 Lucy Maud Montgomery's heroine
3 What Curtis Joseph, Patrick Roy and Martin Brodeur guard
8 Alberta
9 What rowers use
10 Algonquin, Banff, or Spruce Woods
12 People who write poems, i.e. Dennis Lee and Sherri Fitch
13 The Trans Canada _____
14 You could find moles or miners here
15 A great lake and a famous carol
17 An easy way to make someone laugh
20 _____ Trudeau
22 Ed's full name
23 These valuable gems have recently been discovered in northern Canada

DOWN

2 Saskatoon is _____ of Regina
4 A sound that comes back to you
5 A kind of stone that northern carvers often use
6 This fast-paced game is similar to hockey, minus the ice and puck
7 _____ the Turtle, a favourite Canadian book series
9 This grain is often found in porridge
11 B.C.'s famous painter of totem poles and trees, Emily _____
12 A specialty of Prince Edward Island farmers
16 _____ fille
18 The sound that ravens and crows make
19 A nickname for 22 Across
20 A group of whales
21 Toronto's Royal Ontario Museum

Round and Round

This puzzle goes in a spiral, starting with the top left corner and working around until all the spaces are filled up. The start of the next clue is formed by the last one or two letters of the previous answer. The number in brackets at the end of each clue gives the number of letters in the answer.

CLUES

1 Alberta, Saskatchewan and Manitoba (8)
2 What the Inuit used to be called (6)
3 Home to the Expos and the Canadiens (8)
4 Forever (6)
5 A favourite berry (10)
6 A grain crop (3)
7 Capitol of the Northwest Territories (11)
8 A sword sport (7)
9 There are five lakes that are this (5)
10 You have to be one of these to compete in the Canada Games (7)
11 The number of provinces (3)
12 Home to Queen Elizabeth (7)
13 Finished (4)

Canadian Bands

Three of the band names below have been made up. Can you guess who they are?

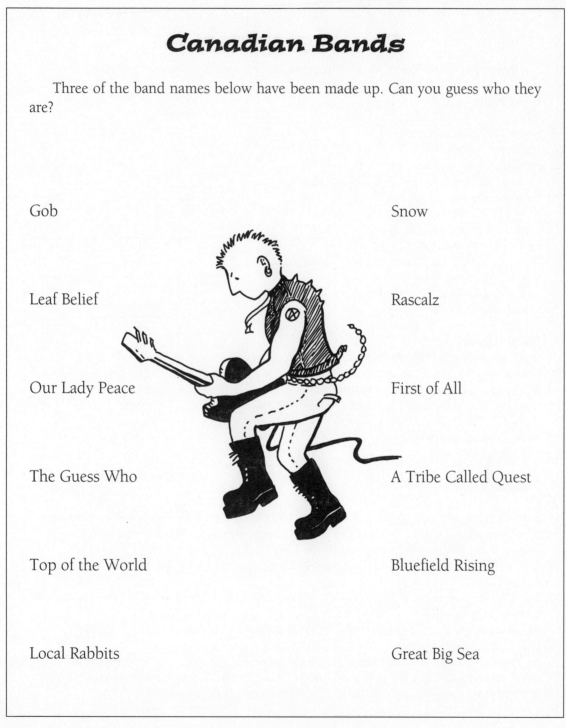

Gob

Snow

Leaf Belief

Rascalz

Our Lady Peace

First of All

The Guess Who

A Tribe Called Quest

Top of the World

Bluefield Rising

Local Rabbits

Great Big Sea

ANSWERS

Please note: To the best of our knowledge, all answers were accurate as of September 2001.

Home Plates (page 7)
Alberta: Wild Rose Country
British Columbia: Beautiful
Manitoba: Friendly
New Brunswick: picture of ship
Newfoundland & Labrador: A World of Difference
Northwest Territories: Explore Canada's Arctic
Nova Scotia: Canada's Ocean Playground
Nunavut: Explore Canada's Arctic
Ontario: Yours to Discover
Prince Edward Island: Confederation Bridge/Birthplace of Confederation
Quebec: Je me souviens
Saskatchewan: Land of Living Skies
Yukon: The Klondike

Dream Teams (page 8)
Regina Redcaps and Brandon Hurricanes are fake.
Toronto Lynx: A-League Soccer; Ottawa Rebel: National Lacrosse League; Edmonton Trappers: Pacific Coast League Baseball; Montreal Alouettes: Canadian Football League; Saint John Flames: American League Hockey; Vancouver Breakers: USL W-1 Women's Soccer League.

Multiple Mounties (page 8)
2 & 5 are the same.

Common Ground (pages 9 & 10)
1) b
2) b: Garneau had NASA flights in 1984, 1996, 2000; Hadfield in 1995 & 2001; Payette in 1999.
3) a: James Naismith invented basketball in 1891, Joseph-Armand Bombardier snowmobiles in 1922, and Zip Gideon Sundback the zipper in 1913.
4) c: Walker plays for the Colorado Rockies, Dempster for the Florida Marlins, and Stairs for the Chicago Cubs.
5) a: Cutrone won in the 3000M Relay in 1992, McKoy in the 110M Hurdles in 1992; Cain in the 1500M Canoe in 1984.
6) a: all three are made of nickel, while the nickel is made of 25% nickel and 75% copper.
7) a: all made by EA Canada.
8) c: Lake Manitoba is home to Manipogo, Okanagan Lake to Ogopogo, and Lake Winnipeg to Winnipogo.
9) a: Trans-Canada is world's longest national highway; Confederation is world's longest bridge stretching over ice-covered water; Rideau is world's longest skating rink.

Record-Makers (page 11)
1) Bruny Surin 2) Simon Whitfield 3) Catriona Le May Doan
4) Sandra Schmirler 5) Elvis Stojko 6) Donovan Bailey

You Live Where? (page 12)
The leftover letters spell
Spring Valley and Autumn Island

O Hungry? O Canada! (page 13)
The leftover letters spell Winter Cove and
Summerland

On Land and Sea (page 15) ———→

What Am I? (pages 16 & 17)
1) Niagara Falls
2) Oak Island
3) Stanley Cup

Spot the Difference: Camping (pages 18 & 19)
• button on boy's jean pocket
• circle on boy's shoe
• boy's cap
• animal prints on backcover of book
• stripes on girl's shoe

Spot the Difference: Camping (cont'd.)
- carrot/banana on blanket
- ant on orange
- toad's spots
- wildflower by toad
- stripe on raccoon's tail
- rabbit's ear
- pocket on backpack
- pocket on tent flap
- worms
- lizard's marking
- snake's tongue
- chipmunk's tail
- caterpillar on tree branch
- butterfly
- owl's feet
- tail of bird on tent
- skunk's tail
- snail

It's a Numbers Game (page 20)
1) 6
2) 6
3) 17,400
4) 30,750,087
5) 5
6) 285
7) 51
8) 63
9) 5,959
10) 178
11) 5
12) 9,984,670

Lost Letters (page 21)
The missing letters spell POLAR BEAR

Lights... Camera... Action! (page 22)
Keanu Reeves: Speed
Jim Carrey: How the Grinch Stole Christmas
Mike Myers: Austin Powers
Neve Campbell: Scream 2
William Shatner: Star Trek, The Final Frontier
Brendan Fraser: The Mummy
Carrie-Anne Moss: Red Planet
Dan Aykroyd: Blues Brother 2000
Leslie Nielsen: Mr. Magoo
Margot Kidder: Superman
Rick Moranis: Honey I Shrunk the Kids
Tom Green: Freddy Got Fingered
Joshua Jackson: The Skulls

Odd One Out (page 23)
Islands: Red Deer
Lakes: Lacrosse
Rivers: Pippen
Mountains: Leisure
Parks: Chitimani
Prime Ministers: Preston Manning
Native Groups: Inukstituk
Birds: Chickaree
Deer: Antler

Olympic Games (pages 24 & 25)
1) c
2) a
3) c
4) a
5) b
6) b

Wild Canada (page 26)
Cardinal, caribou, chickadee, chipmunk, coyote, crane

Dollars and Cents (page 27)
1) quarter
2) nickel
3) dime
4) $1 coin (loonie)
5) penny
6) 50 cent piece
7) $2 coin (toonie)

What's My Sport (pages 28 & 29) ⟶

Prime Time (pages 30 & 31)
1) Rhea: Sabrina
2) William: X-Files
3) Sarah: Scrubs
4) Perry: Friends
5) Cathy: Hour, Minutes
6) Brett: Player
7) Shatner: Star Trek
8) Torrens: Jonovision
9) Joshua: Dawson's
10) Trebeck: Jeopardy!
11) Colin: Line

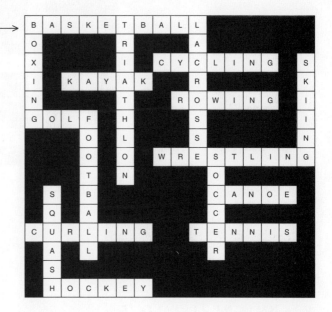

Confused Cities (page 32)
1) Victoria, BC
2) Toronto, ON
3) Montreal, QC
4) Calgary, AB
5) Moncton, NB
6) Halifax, NS
7) Whitehorse, YK
8) Gander, NF
9) Winnipeg, MB
Mystery Word = Saskatoon

Juggled Geography (page 33)

Arctic Circle
Digby Neck
Gros Morne
Lake Louise
Moose Jaw
Peace River
Prince George
Swift Current

Bay of Fundy
Georgian Bay
Hudson Bay
Mont Tremblant
Okanagan Valley
Point Pelee
Riding Mountain
Thousand Islands

Across Canada (pages 34 & 35)——→

Flags (pages 36 & 37)
1) Northwest Territories
2) Nova Scotia
3) Quebec
4) Alberta
5) British Columbia
6) Ontario
7) Saskatchewan
8) Yukon
9) Nunavut
10) New Brunswick
11) Newfoundland & Labrador
12) Manitoba
13) Prince Edward Island

Wild Canada #2 (page 38)
Marmot, mink, mole, moose,
mouse, muskrat

Famous Canadians (page 39)
Missing name = JEAN

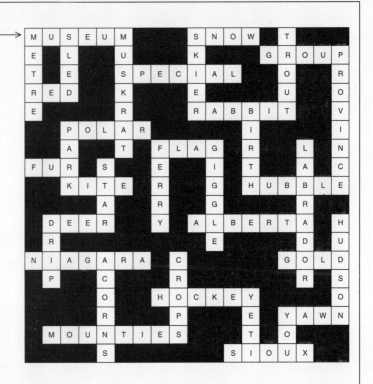

Puzzling Pictures (pages 40 & 41)
1) Medicine Hat
2) Cornwall
3) Manitoba
4) Nunavut
5) Moncton
6) Yellowknife
7) Igloolik
8) Cavendish
9) Burnaby
10) Moose Jaw
11) Coaticook

Who Am I? (pages 42 & 43)
1) Sir John A MacDonald
2) Terry Fox
3) Manon Rheaume

Double Dribble (page 43)
4 & 5 are the same.

Puzzling Letters (page 44)
a) starve
b) large
c) elk
d) tale
Mystery word: GREAT SLAVE LAKE

Lost Letters #2 (page 45)
The missing letters spell MAPLE SYRUP

Your Choice (pages 46 & 47)
1) c
2) b
3) b
4) c
5) b
6) a
7) a
8) c

Across Canada #2
(pages 50 & 51) ──────────→

Boggling Letters (page 52)
We found 24 words:

acorn	cane	care	carve
cave	cone	core	corn
cove	cover	crane	crave
crone	cure	curve	nave
near	over	race	rave
roan	rove	rune	vane

Puzzling Letters #2 (page 53)
a) land
b) skier
c) bears
d) read
Mystery word:
        BARE NAKED LADIES

Spot the Difference: Hockey (pages 48 & 49)
• writing on hockey stick lying on ice
• writing on goalie stick
• vents on helmet lying on ice
• skate logos (2)
• girl's ponytail
• #99 to #66
• goalie hockey jersey (number and logo) (2)
• goalie's skate
• goalie's pads
• #7's stick and socks (2)
• hockey glove on ice
• dog's spots
• shape of dog's tag
• birds
• maple leaf logo on jersey
• tree
• snowshovel by house
• window pane
• tape on stick (behind net)

Weather Wonders (page 54 & 55)
1) c: Yellowknife, where the average annual temperature is -5.1 Celsius.
2) b: the size of an orange.
3) a: Some people climbed down into the dry gorge and picked up bayonets, muskets, tomahawks and swords from the War of 1812. Others crossed the empty river bed on foot or by horse and buggy.
4) a
5) c
6) b
7) False; they are all terms for ice.
8) True

The Doors (pages 56 & 57)
She lives at #101

More Choices (pages 58 & 59)
1) a
2) b
3) c
4) b
5) b
6) c
7) c
8) a
9) c

Canadiana (pages 60 and 61)

Round and Round (page 62)

P	R	A	I	R	I	E	S
E	R	R	Y	E	L	L	K
B	E	A	T	H	L	O	I
W	R	N	D	O	E	W	M
A	G	A	E	N	T	K	O
R	N	L	G	N	E	N	N
T	I	C	N	E	F	I	T
S	Y	A	W	L	A	E	R

Band Names (page 63)
The fake names are Leaf Belief, Top of the World, and Bluefield Rising

About the Authors

Jesse Ross, co-author of the *Amazing Allstar Hockey Activity Book*, is a 15-year-old sports and video game enthusiast. **Ruth Porter**, Jesse's mom, publishes and edits the *Polestar Family Calendar*. They live in B.C.'s Slocan Valley.

They can be contacted at njr@netidea.com

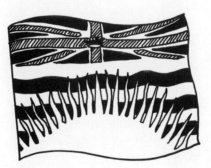